How to Cleanse Spirit Energy
The Step-by-Step Guide to a Heavenly Home
Second Edition

Laine Crosby

How to Cleanse Spirit Energy

The Step-by-Step Guide to a Heavenly Home
Second Edition

Laine Crosby
Published by the Redd Group

Copyright © 2020 Elaine Crosby

ISBN: 978-1-940261-05-8

To Chris, Annie and Caleb

With thanks to Rosemary Ellen Guiley,
Dave Juliano and Patty Wilson.

CONTENTS

FOREWORD

I first met Laine while writing a story for a local travel magazine and was lucky enough to witness her work, investigating spirits in the historic district of Spotsylvania Court House, VA. It was literally a life changing experience for me. Fortunately, for the world, Laine is not only gifted with spiritual abilities, but she is also a talented writer, and is sharing her amazing story with us all, beginning with the fantastic, *Investigative Medium–the Awakening*. Her latest work, *How to Cleanse Spirit Energy: The Step-by-Step Guide to a Heavenly Home* is a must read. Yes, it offers a detailed and practical framework for those with unwanted spirits in need of cleansing, but it is also a fascinating look at understanding spirit energy, and is filled with enlightening and sometimes entertaining stories that help expand our awareness of a world that surrounds us every day.

– J.S. Campbell, author of *A Year of Critical Thinking*

OPENING REMARKS

I'll never forget going to my daughter's fourth grade winter concert and listening to the other moms talk about their Christmas vacation. The O'Brians went to Walt Disney World, the Webbs went to Ocean City, and then it was my turn. I didn't think my husband would approve if I told these women I performed an exorcism, but I would have enjoyed seeing their faces, if I had shared. I paused as I contemplated how much to say.

"Oh, you know, we celebrated Christmas, visited some historic sites—the usual." They all turned back to their conversation—not really knowing how to respond to such a sad, uneventful story. But that's the story of my life. My closest friends love to hear about my adventures, but sometimes, I have had to leave reality at the door for the good of my children, parochial school, and those who may not want their kids playing with a child who sees ghosts and doesn't even care.

I have been known to take my children to swim practice, then rush off for clandestine work, and return to make pancakes with whipped cream smiley faces by morning. I live the most honestly deceitful life I know. And I love every minute of it.

If you've read my book, *Investigative Medium –the Awakening*, you know I live in a new house on an old plantation. And you know the horror of our first months here, discovering I was suddenly psychic, and learning to cleanse my house. It was a hard time for us all. The spirits didn't necessarily come with the house, but when word got out that I could hear and feel them, they came from all around to get my attention. In other words, I was haunted. And my husband and children began having experiences as well.

Many have told me similar stories of unwanted hauntings, and they had nowhere to turn for help. I learned how to take control of my house, and I hope this guide will make it easier for others to do so also. The first version of this guide was originally a blog that I wrote in response to a number of emails I received after my first show aired on the Travel Channel. Usually, the conversation began with, "You are going to think I am crazy, but…" I thought, "If they only knew what I've been through, they would never say that!"

I spoke with teachers, doctors, FBI agents, military personnel, preachers, mothers, plumbers, contractors, and even the head of IT for a clandestine government agency. None of these folks dared to mention their situation to anyone else, for fear of sounding "crazy." However, the paranormal is part of our everyday lives, whether we acknowledge it or not.

I am now an Investigative Medium, and I work with historians, authors, archaeologists, and law enforcement to find out what history has not revealed. I talk to spirits—folks just like you and me—and I listen to their stories of life and death. I hear about history from those who lived it, and I write and lecture about my findings.

In my work as an Investigative Medium, I have dealt with malevolent entities from time to time. Sometimes they center around murder cases, and often times they will be at locations such as jails, prisons, and where enslaved people experienced pain. I learned how to handle these situations, cross over ghosts who remained, and cleanse locations of residual energy or malevolent spirits. In theory, I exorcised these locations of negative energy.

Exorcism is not just a Catholic ritual. While the Catholic Church says that the adjuration of negative spirits in the name of God or Christ is strictly a religious act or rite, the earliest evidence of exorcisms pre-date Christianity by hundreds of years.[1] Exorcism is often misunderstood in today's media-influenced culture, but Demonologist Dave Juliano says it simply means "to clear or expel by, or as if by incantation, command or prayer."[2]

The Catholic Church, goes a step further to say exorcism is "(1) the act of driving out, or warding off, demons, or evil spirits, from persons, places, or things, which are believed to be possessed or infested by them, or are liable to become victims or instruments of their malice; (2) the means employed for this purpose, especially the solemn

---

[1]https://www.metmuseum.org/exhibitions/listings/2014/assyria-to-iberia/blog/posts/pazuzu, Pazuzu: Beyond Good and Evil, September 29, 2014, by Sarah Graff, Associate Curator, Department of Ancient Near Eastern Art

[2] *Armor of God: Prayers for Protection and Deliverance* by Dave Juliano, page 8.

and authoritative adjuration of the demon, in the name of God, or any of the higher power in which he is subject."[3]

Put simply, exorcism is the expulsion of an unwanted force or energy from a person, place, or thing that is afflicted by that energy. In the extreme, a person who is possessed by such a force loses self-control as a result of that possession. An exorcist is a person who specializes in casting out these entities. So if you or anyone you know is not a linguist but begins to speak Latin, and is prone to levitation, an exorcist could be helpful. And a psychiatrist.

I would like to draw a distinction between what I describe in this book about cleansing a location, and the exorcism of a person. Cleansing locations to remove unwanted, residual, or negative energy and demonic entities, is very different from exorcising a demon out of a person. When there is a case of demonic possession, a number of signs progress over time. When people approach me whom I believe may be involved in a valid case of

---

[3] *The Catholic Encyclopedia*, http://www.newadvent.org/cathen/05709a.htm

possession, I refer them to a demonologist for further exploration and action. (See Chapter 3 on malevolent entities.)

As a Methodist, I recite in the Apostles Creed, "I believe in the Holy Spirit, the Holy Catholic Church, the communion of Saints, the forgiveness of sins, the resurrection of the body, and the life everlasting." And therefore, I often use Catholic prayers, call on the spirits of saints, priests, and angels, for assistance. The Catholic Church has an arm which deals with demonic possession, and I do believe they have the most widely known, used, and established protocol. And for this reason, I often use Catholic prayers and practices when cleansing a home.

However, while I am a Christian and personally rely on the Holy Trinity, please do not make the mistake to think that I am forcing my belief system on anyone who is not a Christian. Almost all religions have some form of exorcism, and each religion has their own way of asking for protection from God. Most resemble each other, even though the name used for God may be Yahweh, Allah, Vishnu or many others. While the religious history and backstory may be different, the principles are similar.

Before beginning your cleansing, I highly recommend buying *Armor of God: Prayers for Protection and Deliverance* by Dave Juliano.[4] It is available on Amazon in paperback as well as an ebook. This is the best publication I have found that includes prayers from various religions. When you do the cleansing I discuss in the next chapters, you will want to have prayers available, and this book is my "go-to." I have a copy in my bedroom, my office, and in my "to go" bag in my car. I have also included additional prayers and scripture in Chapter 9.

Earlier this year I filmed an episode of *Ghost Brothers: Haunted Houseguests* for the Travel Channel, which is the fourth episode of season one of the series, entitled "Demon Problems." I cleansed a home with a number of low-level demonic entities in the episode. While I did a lot of shouting in this episode, this is *not* how I recommend you cleanse a house in every circumstance. Like angels, there is a hierarchy of demonic entities, and they respond in different ways.

---

[4] https://www.amazon.com/s?
k=Dave+Juliano&ref=nb_sb_noss_2

Some may run when confronted loudly, and others will use that energy to manifest more, and cling to you. The reason I chose to raise my voice at times is because I have guides who directed me to do so. I would *not* recommend that anyone who is not sensitive do so, as it could be a more combative approach. However, I had the camera crew between the entity and me, and I had to be efficient to ensure they were safe too. I found that when I yelled, the strong entity retreated, just as my spirit guides had said it would.

In cleansing the home, I used several tactics, but since the cleansing lasted six hours, only a portion could be seen on the show. Not all cleansings take this long. A house of the same size typically takes about an hour for me, but in this case there was a large infestation of negative entities.

Here you'll find a step-by-step method for cleansing spirit energy, and dealing with entities who respond in various ways. The information in this book comes from years of experience helping others, what my spirit guides have taught me, and what I have learned from friends Rosemary Ellen Guiley, Dave Juliano, Patty A. Wilson, and John Zaffis. I revised this second edition of *How to Cleanse Spirit Energy* based on reader feedback, and this book now includes:

- Greater explanations and background;
- How-to information for crossing over ghosts;
- Prayers of protection; and
- References for more information.

I hope you will find it helpful. If you have any specific questions, you may reach me through my website at LaineCrosby.com. You may also want to read *Investigative Medium–the Awakening*, the story of the spirits in my home, how my family and I managed, and what we learned. Thank you for reading my guide to cleansing spirit energy, and good luck!

1.

UNDERSTANDING ENERGY

When you walk into a room where there has been an argument, you may be able to sense how differently the room feels. When a friend is angry or upset, you may be able to feel that too. Our emotions are energy, and we can leave behind this energy.

When I use the term "energy," this can be ghosts or spirits, or emotions or feelings. Positive energy and positive thoughts attract positive energy, and negative thoughts (and actions) attract negative energy. This is not necessarily ghosts, and it is not necessarily demons. It is parasitic energy that is attracted to another energy source to live. It can also wander in with guests, contractors, or those who may service or visit your home. Many people assign names to this energy, but in essence, everything is simply energy–negative or positive energy, with or without intelligence.

If you are moving into a new house, you may want to remove the energy of anything that happened before you arrived. It's always a good idea to cleanse your home whether you've lived in it for years or are just moving in, although rarely do people do this unless they find themselves with a haunting.

"Hurry and get over here! I have a demon in my closet!" If you've sent me an email with this line as the subject, take a deep breath. First of all, when you are sensitive, energies, entities, or ghosts may feel malevolent to you. Only with experience comes discernment, so please don't jump to conclusions if you are scared. Ninety-nine out of a hundred times, that scary thing in your closet is just a ghost, or the air conditioning unit. Just because something makes the hair stand up on your neck, does not mean it is bad. How would you feel if you died and someone started screaming and chasing you with sage? Ghosts are people too.

Second, asking me for help won't do the trick. I can come over and get rid of your ghosts, demons, negative energy and all the scary stuff, but it is your house and they know it. If you have a haunting and you let someone else cleanse your house, it won't help you in the long run. The spirits will realize you are not in control of your own house, and as a result, they won't take you seriously, and they will return. You have to take control and do the cleansing yourself for it to work. Or, at least be part of the process and demand that the energy or spirits leave. You can have someone sensitive with you if you need help feeling the change in energy, but ultimately, you have the responsibility to get the job done right. And, if you are doing a cleansing, my guess is that you are sensitive yourself and that's why you feel you need to cleanse. Ministers and priests can also help if you feel more inclined, but you must be the one to take control and keep control.

Control is the most important part of the process of expelling anything or anyone unwanted from your home. If your will is firm and unyielding, the energy will leave. If you are scared because you hear voices, see shadows, or feel things that go bump in the night, you need to tell the ghosts that they bother you and they must leave you alone.

Be firm but not outraged; you don't want them to become indignant. Remind them that it is your home and ask them to respect your wishes. Ghosts will most likely leave when you ask them to do so, or they will stay out of your way so you won't notice them as much.

However, I've had some ghosts who were more problematic than demonic entities. Jerks don't become nice just because they are dead. I discuss how I have handled these in Chapter 5, "Cautionary Tales."

In one of the most widely known scriptures, Matthew 17:20, Jesus said, "… Truly I tell you, if you have faith like a grain of mustard seed, you can say to this mountain, 'Move from here to there,' and it will move. Nothing will be impossible for you." When we pray for protection and for spiritual works, we will receive them, if only we believe we will. Simply saying a prayer isn't enough. We must have intention combined with faith to move mountains—or negative entities, as the case may be. And again—believe—even if you don't call the supreme power of the universe "Christ." As long as you don't call it "Satan," the big guy's got you covered.

2.

GHOSTS AND SPIRITS

"Spirits" is an umbrella term to mean souls or supernatural beings who are not in physical form, which also includes ghosts. To make it easy for everyone, I use the term "ghosts" to mean those human (or animal) souls that have not crossed over into Heaven, but have remained in this physical dimension after death. Most often, I use the term "spirit" or "spirits" to refer to souls who have crossed over. Technically, ghosts are spirits, but this terminology will keep it simple.

Jesus Christ explained in John 4:24, "God is Spirit." Spiritualists[5]—and many folks these days—use "Spirit" as a plural to describe all minds and positive entities who are in the spirit world,

---

[5] *A spiritualist church is a church affiliated with the informal spiritualist movement which began in the United States in the 1840s. Lilydale Assembly in Lilydale, New York is world's largest center for the science, philosophy and religion of Spiritualism, beginning in1879. The Spiritualist Church is dedicated to the service of God, Spirit and mankind—the foundation upon which all else is built. Spiritualists believe as do many of all faiths, that after death, we continue to exist on a spiritual plane. Church services are usually conducted by a medium, and there is prayer, an address, singing of hymns, and a "demonstration of mediumship." This demonstration is basically a medium or mediums, reading those in attendance.* https://lilydaleassembly.org/about-us/

including God. I hear this more and more, and I want to say you won't hear it from me, unless it's a typo. I am a writer and I just can't use a singular noun as a plural. Because I'm teaching you how to fight or cleanse, I'll be more specific so you'll have a greater tactical understanding.

When we die, we can move on, cross over into another dimension or plane, or we can stay here. It is always our choice. No one is ever trapped; entrapments are only perceived. Our perceptions in life are based on our life experiences, and our faith is based on experience or upbringing, too. We may be Christian, Jewish, Buddhist or Muslim, because we were born into a family with these beliefs. We may doubt the presence of God when we experience a crisis or when someone we love dies. Our perceptions are molded by these experiences.

Companies know that a consumer's perception is his or her reality. That's why businesses build brands, to give customers an experience that will shape their opinion. If customers experience a brand positively, that brand becomes their only choice–not that it is the only choice–but companies want customers to perceive it is. Creating a brand and positive brand experience is the most important job of a marketer. It costs far more to change customer perception than it does to create a new product and brand benefits. If you don't believe me, just ask Tylenol, Toyota, or Coca-Cola.

Or, you can find out yourself from a ghost. Time and time again, spirits have told me four main reasons they remain on earth rather than crossing over into Heaven:

1. Some have died traumatic deaths and don't know they are dead.

2. Some believe God won't take them because their sins are horrific. They are afraid if they try to cross over, they will be sent to Hell.

3. Some souls don't believe in God, so they don't believe there is a Heaven, and they may wander the earth.

4. And, some souls refuse to cross over because everyone they know is here, so they won't leave to pursue the unknown.

However, inherent in this rationale is a single overarching reason why ghosts remain. They stay because they identify with their physical nature so much that they view themselves only as physical beings. Then, through death, they become spiritual beings. When people understand their spiritual nature, it is their expectation to go home to the spirit world after death. However, when people do not view themselves as a spiritual beings, they cling to the material nature of the physical world and do not want to move on. I learned as a brand marketer that it is far easier to create perceptions than to change perceptions, and it is the case here. It's not always easy to convince ghosts they should move on, and give up the ghost.

3.

MALEVOLENT ENTITIES

In ancient times, demons and the demonic realm were thought of very differently than they are now in the modern West. There is much demon lore in the anthologies of the ancient Hebrews, Egyptians, Greeks, Romans, Assyrians, Persians and other cultures. "Demons" included a wide range of spirits, both tricky and evil, and they caused all sorts of problems for people, including the ills of the world. These demons included low-level problematic entities and also those who wielded enormous power and had the ability to wreak havoc.

These beings exist alongside us in inter-dimensional space, and they continue to pose problems. They have changed their form and tactics as humans have changed throughout time.

Religions and Demonic Entities

Harper's Encyclopedia of Mystical and Paranormal Experience by Rosemary Ellen Guiley discusses various religions and their practices:

"Christianity associates exorcism with demonic possession, which is believed to be caused by Satan. The exorcism is considered to be the battle for the victim's soul. Only the Roman Catholics offer a formal rite of exorcism: the *Ritual Romanum,* dating back to 1614. Before the rite can be performed, certain symptoms must manifest, such as levitation, superhuman strength, clairvoyance, the foreswearing of all religious words or articles, or speaking in tongues. The rite is characterized by violence: the victim suffers pain, extraordinary contortions, disgusting body noises, diarrhea, spitting, vomiting, and swearing. The room may be plunged alternately into heat or cold, and objects make fly about.

Some Protestants perform exorcisms as well. The Pentecostals and other charismatics practice "deliverance ministry," where gifted people drive out devils and heal through the laying on of hands. In Judaism, rabbinical literature dating to the first century refers to exorcism rituals. Perhaps the best known rite concerns the dybbuk, an evil spirit or doomed soul that possesses the soul of the victim and causes mental illness and a personality change… In Hinduism, Buddhism, Islam, and

Shinto, and many other religions, spirits and ghosts are routinely blamed for a host of ills and are cast out of people and places. Most such afflictions are not considered all-or-nothing battles for souls…In some Shamanic traditions, it is believed that demons or spirits cause maladies and misfortune by stealing souls."

It may surprise you to know that even Satanists have exorcisms. Demons, are thought to be three different entities, rather than demons. The first type of entities are pagan deities they believe have literally been demonized by the Church. The second type is a chaotic force. These are more like natural forces–they don't have a sense of good and evil as we understand it. The third type is a thought form that humans bring into existence though their own energy and will.[6]

While almost all world religions have their own versions of exorcism, they do not all use the same terminology. Negative energy has many forms. Everything comes back to energy, so an entity can appear as a beetle, or a wolf,

---

[6] https://www.vice.com/en_us/article/4354zp/these-occult-exorcists-say-the-catholic-church-makes-demons-worse

a djinn,[7] a vampire, or simply just a strange shape or half-animal, half-human. It can also look like electricity, like a dog or mist. How people see this energy may vary according to their beliefs, perspective, or how an entity would like to be seen. For example, if you believe in Voodoo, you may see a loa.[8] The entities present themselves as such to be understood and affect the possessed.[9]

Types of Demonic Possession

Everywhere I turn, television shows and movies talk about "demons" because it is perceived to be a scary topic that will engage audiences. It sounds a lot more terrifying than "negative entity," right? I've included this section in reference to "demons"—not because it is common—but because you'll see it on television and the movies. The six types of demonic attacks (also called six types of possession) are:

1. *Oppression.* A demon torments a person causing tragic events in their life, such as

---

[7] https://www.britannica.com/topic/jinni

[8] https://www.britannica.com/topic/lwa-Vodou

[9] https://www.vice.com/en_us/article/4354zp/these-occult-exorcists-say-the-catholic-church-makes-demons-worse

the loss of a loved one, a job, or a home. (e.g. the book of *Job*.)

2. *Infestation.* Demonic entities increase in number and torment those in a home.

3. *Physical Pain.* Sickness or injury is due to a demon which affects the physical body, not the soul.

4. *Possession.* A demon or demons take over a person's body without their consent. This is what you see in most movies. It involves a change in personality, speaking in tongues, sudden violence, and even sometimes super-human strength.

5. *Subjugation.* A person invites a demonic entity into their life. This can be through game playing (Ouija), or through literally inviting a demon into their life. If a human wants power, they can trade the future for their soul.

6. *Obsession.* A person has constant and overwhelming irrational thoughts making them act in adverse ways. This is difficult to detect and can lead to suicide.

Typically, the endgame of a demon is possession. It always starts small. Someone used a Ouija

Board. Or, someone takes drugs and drinks excessively, and isn't in a happy, sober state of mind. Or, something malevolent follows from a cemetery. Or, negative emotions and unhappiness linger. Then it grows over time. No happy, spiritually-connected person, who does not seek out paranormal activity or the dark side, is going to become possessed. And no one becomes possessed overnight, just like one bite of cake isn't going to change your waistline by morning. But if you continue eating lots of cake, you may end up with excess weight, organ failure, and diabetes.

Some find dabbling in the paranormal hard to resist, and sensitive people need to be more careful. As I've said, spirits come to those they know can feel them, so if you are sensitive, you'll have to be extra vigilant with protection.

4.

ATTACHMENTS

In addition to people and locations, physical objects can also be haunted. They can have residue and attachments that become problematic. People and objects can also be haunted by negative entities as well as human dead who are angry or unhappy. I have come across hundreds if not thousands of haunted objects. In fact, Demonologist John Zaffis has come across so many that he now has a museum in a barn on his property, "John's Museum of the Paranormal," where he houses possessed objects he receives.

The following stories are examples of attachments I've experienced, and how I have handled their removal.

The Portal.

When filming *Ghost Brothers: Haunted Houseguests*, the homeowner, Lori, had a large mirror that had an attachment. I learned from John Zaffis that mirrors can be doorways for spirits to enter the world.[10] On the way to the airport to go home, I began to review in my mind what happened over the last week of filming. One thing that stood out to me was how sensitive Lori was. She was able to tell me where entities were, and she was always right. She had also commented in passing that her sister always cried when she slept in the room with the mirror. I recalled that it taunted me and tried to make me cry.

Then it hit me! I immediately called our executive producer to let him know that one of the more frustrating demons had been attached to the mirror, and it needed to be moved to the barn right away. Thankfully they got rid of it that day, but after hearing me talk with the producer, I don't know if my cab driver could sleep that night.

The Businessman.

The Rising Sun Tavern is owned by the National Trust for Historic Preservation and it is located at 1304 Caroline St., Historic District, Fredericksburg, Virginia. In 1760, George Washington's brother

---

[10] Demon Haunted: True Stories from the John Zaffis Vault Kindle Edition by John Zaffis and Rosemary Ellen Guiley, page 11.

Charles originally built the tavern as his home. The curator asked me to visit to tell them more about the spirits there, and the unknown history. I was told by the ghosts that it was a watering hole for Patrick Henry, James Madison, and even George Washington. If you take the tour, you'll hear about many more famous politicians who visited here, as well.

I saw a beautiful desk in the lobby, and it was made by a well-known craftsman of the eighteenth century. I had read about this craftsman in the Daughters of the American Revolution magazine, so I laid my hands on the desk to see if I could perceive more about its origins. When I did so, I sensed the man who owned the desk was still attached to it. He told me he had saved money most of his life to commission the desk from the original craftsman. Apparently, he spent a lot of time here, mulling over the finances of his farm and businesses. I could tell that when people complimented the desk, he felt as if he himself were the object of affection. The desk was also a symbol for what he loved to do most in life, and he would not let go.

The Skull.

After my friend Branden moved into a Gettysburg

home with his wife and daughter, he mentioned that something felt strange in his house. He didn't know quite what it was that felt "off," but he trusted his feeling. Since he is a contractor, he was constantly making renovations, so naturally, I wasn't sure whether the renovations were creating issues, or if he felt fallen soldiers from the Battle of Gettysburg.

When I visited him, I found that neither were the case. At first I thought the issue may have been the Lenni Lenape peoples, whose chief, Sosundi, spoke with me. Because the tribe had lived in the 1800s, they had also learned English from the settlers and were a friendly group. I enjoyed my conversations with Sosundi and thought maybe Branden was picking up on his thoughts. But as time passed, Branden's dreams grew more sinister.

One night Branden had a very vivid dream of being chased by a tiger. Another night, that tiger morphed into several other cryptid-like creatures, each more scary than the one before. I cleansed a second time, but the dreams continued. Then, the entity became emboldened. One night Branden and Mary were in their bedroom, and they saw a cantaloupe-sized swirling ball of light appear in front of them. The inside of the ball was moving, like bacteria in a petrie dish. It hovered over them for a while and then disappeared. The haunting had now escalated, and the entity was also witnessed by his wife.

I returned soon after that incident and was having lunch with Mary in the kitchen. I noticed there was the skull of a cow, hung high up on a wall nearby. In fact, there was a collection of skulls. I focused and knew right away that one of them had an attachment. Mary explained that Branden flew small aircraft with his father, and they would find these in the desert and bring them back. "Boys and their toys," I thought, and then I became distracted and didn't give it a second thought. That is, until I ran into Branden at his mom's farm soon after. He told me the dreams had gotten better for a while after my last cleansing, but they were back. I casually mentioned that objects can also be haunted, and I reiterated what I had told Mary about the skull. At the time, I didn't realize a haunting of this magnitude could be caused by this possessed possession. Mea culpa.

Branden is a burly hunter, whom I doubt is afraid of much. He's also very sensitive and often sees ghosts at his mother's farm down the road. While I've been asked by frightened

Marines to help with lesser matters, I felt Branden could handle whatever was happening. I was there to help figure it out so he would know what to do to get it to leave.

The next time I visited his mother, I noticed a cow skull hung on the door of her barn. And after Branden moved it there, he never had any more problems in his house. Now the barn is a different story…

The Possessed Doll.

The Richard Johnson Inn is a beautiful, historic inn, in Fredericksburg, Virginia. I was on an investigative weekend with Mark and Carol Nesbitt, Patty Wilson, Brad Christman, and a group who came for the adventure. After I checked in, I climbed the stairs from the foyer to the second floor and saw my room was one of two rooms on that level. It was quiet and we were separated from all of the other rooms on the far side of the inn. I turned the key in the lock, dropped my bags, and lay down on the bed to rest before my lecture and investigation. As I relaxed, I felt someone watching me. I opened my eyes to see there was a doll in my room. Not much surprises me, but I have never liked dolls, and this was unsettling. This particular doll was especially creepy because it had huge feet.

I was determined to get the doll out of my room. At dinner, two paranormal investigators enthusiastically volunteered to put the doll in their room, which was separated only by a thin wall. Against my better judgment, I told them to "go for it." I was happy to have it out of my room. They talked to it for hours and even recorded EVP from it that said "My feet not big." It definitely had an attachment.

I cleansed my room as I describe in Chapter 6. I used holy water on the walls and over the door, in the sign of the cross. Then, I went to bed. The next morning the two ladies with the doll were exhausted and dragged themselves to breakfast. They asked, "Did you hear the commotion in the hall outside our rooms all night?" They told me that they were afraid to open the door because people were banging on the walls, yelling, and falling down the stairs. They presumed that drunk fraternity boys from Mary Washington University must have ventured through an unlocked door. Although I'm a light sleeper, it was one of my most peaceful nights of sleep. No one in the inn heard anything unusual that night, except these ladies.

I took the doll to the innkeeper and suggested she throw it in the river. I'm sure it could have been cleansed, but since I'm not a fan of creepy dolls to begin with, I wasn't going out of my way. It was so ugly, I was sure it would attract another attachment. I later learned that my friend Brad Christman begged the innkeeper for the doll, so he could secretly return it to my room!

The Halloween Dress.

It may have been a dress for a witches costume, but I liked it anyway. It hung on the sale rack at Target, and so I plopped it in my cart without even trying it on. My daughter Annie saw it the next day and asked for first dibs. A few minutes later, she tossed it from her loft, down into the living room. "What's the matter?" I asked.

"It has an attachment," she replied. I felt the dress and put it in the washing machine to save me the trouble of dealing with the attachment. It didn't work. Once clean, the attachment was still on it, and I tossed it in the trash.

The Antique Dealer.

Warren County, North Carolina was the playground of the rich and famous during the great war. Not World War I mind you, but the War Between the States. The war that changed the revenue model for all of the folks there who had mansions on their plantations, as well as mansions in town. Now, within the borders of Warrenton—the county seat—there are a handful of restaurants and a couple thousand of the nicest people you'll ever meet.

Rose and Bob are two of these nice folks. They have lived in the Somerville-Graham House since 2009, and they love Halloween. How could they not, when everyday is Halloween in their haunted abode? The couple graciously invited me for a visit last summer so I could talk to their ghosts and gather stories to add to my lecture and walking tour of the town.

Ferns overflowed on the porch of their bright yellow manor, and the yard was a maze of well-manicured boxwood hedges. I had stepped back in time. I knew many ghosts filled the stately home, so I had to choose my tete-a-tetes wisely; I had little time to talk with everyone on this visit. As Bob opened the front door, I was also greeted by the spirit of a woman named Marnie Scott. Bob and Rose didn't know Marnie, but she had moved in and was there to stay. She told me she arrived with a silver pin that Rose had purchased.

Marnie showed me in my mind that it had silver plumes sticking out from the base. "I already sold that pin," Rose told me. "That doesn't mean that Marnie went with it," I replied.

Marnie was a talker. She told me all about her family–the Morrises–of Mt. Pisgah, North Carolina. She also loved that pin. However, when she had to choose between going with the pin's next owner, or staying, she made the wise choice–remaining in Rose's beautiful antebellum mansion.

Soon, the spirit of previous owner, Helen Franklin, showed up and was quite upset about all the ghosts that were in "her" home. Helen shared lots of information about the other ghosts. Some she could endure, but some caused all kinds of trouble.

There was a room upstairs with beautiful dresses, and Helen remarked that she stays out of "that" room, and she pointed to the door.

The moment I stepped in, I couldn't breathe. Rose began to tell me about the dresses, which she acquired from the Smithsonian Institution. I felt dizzy when I stepped toward the dresses, so I stayed close to the exit. My friend Brooke was by my side, taking notes. She didn't feel disturbed, and neither did Rose. Clearly, the energy—or ghosts attached to the dresses—was only bothering me.

Since the attachments affected no one in the home, I felt that further action by me would only cause problems that didn't exist before. And, because Rose is an antique dealer, if I cleansed the house, more would continue to come with antiques and visitors.

Rose and Bob open their beautiful home each year on Halloween for a tour, and souls from far and wide come to see the decorations. And, I have no doubt that most of them float through the front door.

Attachments to Those Who Are Sensitive and Those with Special Needs.

Having Aspergers, my son Caleb would pick up attachments at school from other special needs students when he was young. My husband teaches special education, and he also comes home with attachments regularly. While a ghost can also attach itself to a person, more commonly it is emotions, feelings and other parasitic energy both negative or positive, that can attach. Mostly, we notice the negative, or how a room or object feels.

I am so empathic that I do a personal cleanse when I go to a restaurant, grocery store, or other place with a lot of people. However, my daughter and I have also had attachments enter our car while driving through town. My son and husband feel them too, mostly when we are driving in populated areas.

There is a church on our street with a parking lot where I took Annie to learn to drive. We went there three times and got an attachment with a headache each time, so we now steer clear of that location. Immediately when we feel the mood change in the car, we tell it to take a hike. It's a lot easier to address it immediately than to do bioenergy, reiki, or prayer removal once it has attached more.

The Backyard Man.
My family and I live in a relatively new house on an old plantation. When my twins were about seven- or eight-years-old, I encountered the spirit of a man who refused to leave us alone. I noticed that my son Caleb was having more meltdowns than usual, but I didn't make the connection right away that a spirit was involved.

Annie, Caleb and I were playing in the living room one day when Annie suddenly said, "There is a man here. He died in a fire." "Annie," I asked, did you hear him tell you that?" "No Mommy," she said, "I just felt that." I felt energy on Caleb's shoulder and I said prayers to get rid of him. But the story doesn't end there.

While Caleb no longer had an attachment and was feeling better, it had not completely left us. The next day I went to Gettysburg for an investigative weekend with my team. At dinner, I mentioned to Patty Wilson that I had a stubborn attachment, and I asked her to help. We went to the bathroom so we wouldn't scare the other folks who had come to investigate with us.

Since the attachment had not let me sleep much the night before, I was tired. And, I refused to have a conversation with it; I didn't want to fuel it with my emotions. Patty focused and said it was a man who had died in a fire. I then knew he was the backyard man. I asked aloud why he was there and why he would attach himself to a sweet little boy. Patty listened and replied, "He says it is okay because something isn't right about Caleb." I was furious, yet I didn't want to yell at him and give him more reason to stick around.

We told him we could help him get to Heaven. He said he didn't believe in God, so there was nowhere to go. We commanded he leave. And, we commanded him again. We prayed. We argued with him. But still, he refused to leave. Then Patty said a prayer like no other. She called on God and asked for angels to come and take away this soul to another dimension—another place of God's choosing where it could not come back and bother us again. After praying for a minute or so, there was a buzz of energy, and then everything felt better. He was gone.

I learned a lesson from Patty that day, a lesson that would serve me time and again over the next decade. We get the spiritual gifts we ask for; we just have to know what to ask.

Be Aware

Attachments can be found anywhere. These are just a few examples; the lesson is to stay open and trust your instincts. Be aware of how objects feel before you bring them home. And cleanse! If you love an antique, it's always easier to cleanse one before you get it in your house. (Or, don't buy it!)

5.

CAUTIONARY TALES

Are you curious about who or what is in your home that is causing a ruckus or feels different? Most people are. Many times I've received "911" calls about problems, and the homeowner wants to know who it is causing the issue and why. It makes sense, if you know why you have a haunting, you can deal with it better. Every case is different, but unless you are psychic, do not be tempted to talk to these entities and find out yourself.

Years ago, I gave homeowners what they wanted—knowledge. People would call me and act terrified, then when I arrived they would say, "You're not going to make them leave, are you?" I was a novelty and they wanted a Broadway Show. Folks, ghosts are not pets. Ever feed a stray cat? Where there is a lot of ghostly activity, and when you speak to your ghosts and use technology to find out who they are and what they want, they'll never leave. And, more will come. If you already have problems, Please don't make the mistake of trying to find out answers simply because it interests you.

Paranormal Investigations of Troubled Homes

If you have a problematic haunting, please do not call a group of investigators or ghost hunters. Most likely, this will cause more activity from the spirits there, and you want to calm down the activity, not the opposite. I am not condemning paranormal investigators or investigations. I have done my share, and I work with some of the best groups out there. However, if you have problems to begin with, don't do anything to stir up more.

Although there are paranormal investigators who are psychic, typically, they are not and do not claim to be. Their job is mainly to look for paranormal anomalies. You may get some good information from Electronic Voice Phenomena (EVP) or a spirit box. But when the investigators leave to return to their own homes, you pay a price. Using these devices in a home that already needs cleansing—and I assume this is the case since you are reading this book–can cause all sorts of problems. And, if someone or something follows them there, or they call in a negative entity by mistake, they may not know it's there or how to get rid of it. You'll be the one to find out. Ghosts like talking to people, and when people communicate with them, they will get excited and more will come.

I made the mistake of having investigators in my own home when I first became psychic, and my family and I were all seeing apparitions after the investigation. As I wrote about in *Investigative Medium–the Awakening*, my home then became out of control in many more ways, with entities talking through toys without batteries, and even through my daughter Annie, who was four-years-old at the time. Believe me, I know what I'm talking about.

Put aside your curiosity and do the cleanse as instructed. If you are cleansing your home to change the energy, or because you have a new home, you don't need to talk to them and stir up things that were not previously problematic If after the cleansing you continue to have issues (as in the case of my friend Branden in Chapter 4), you may want extra help. You'll need a psychic medium or a good sensitive for this, rather than a paranormal investigator who is not sensitive. Make sure you choose someone who is experienced, who can also talk to ghosts or guides and hear or sense their answers, without using any devices. In some cases, you may even need a demonologist. Demonologists are also psychic and specialize in helping people with possessions and serious issues, but you'll need to keep journals and documentation, and you may have a long wait.

These cautionary tales may help so that you don't have some of the same haunted happenings as I have experienced.

The Paranormal Investigators Who Didn't Notice the Ghosts.

On our team's paranormal weekends in Gettysburg, Patty Wilson and I would stay at Mark and Carol Nesbitt's haunted home. It is located at 271 Baltimore Street, and is headquarters to Mark Nesbitt's Ghosts of Gettysburg Candlelight Walking tours. Mrs. Kitzmiller is the spirit who lives upstairs at the tour headquarters. She is a formal lady who died around 1920 and is buried down the street in the National Cemetery. She is especially fond of Patty, who can do no wrong in her eyes.

Mrs. Kitzmiller usually greeted Patty and me upon arrival, but not on this particular Friday. I didn't think anything of it, and I went my separate way to stay in the carriage house. Before the evening's investigation, Patty tried to talk to Mrs. Kitzmiller, but she was wasn't interested in talking. She was furious with us.

Patty and I had been so busy that neither one of us noticed that there was the spirit of a short, stout Italian woman also there. She would not leave, and Mrs. Kitzmiller wanted her out of the house.

"How can you both say you are mediums and not see that woman who refuses to get out of my house?" She demanded.

We talked to the little lady and she said she had nowhere to go. We learned from her that the paranormal investigators had no idea she had followed them from another investigation, stayed with one of them for weeks, then followed them to this location. Nor did they know Mrs. Kitzmiller was there.

We told the unwanted guest that she had to leave, and we tried to cross her over into Heaven, but she would have no part of it. The next day when I left town, she was still standing on the corner of Baltimore and Breckenridge Streets, not knowing where to go. I sent her to the Farnsworth House in the next block, where she wouldn't have to worry about anyone knowing she was there.

Ouija Boards

I have been called repeatedly by people with personal or household hauntings, and a majority of the time, it can be traced back to someone using a Ouija Board, even decades before.

Don't even think about it. Not at home, not at a Bed and Breakfast, not in a field—nowhere. I cannot tell you how many people have had demonic entities enter their homes and their lives, simply by playing with one of these. Using a Ouija Board is like opening your front door and inviting anyone to come in your house and do whatever they want for as long as they like. You have no idea who is lurking in the bushes. You have no idea what spirits may be at the location where you are, nor what spirits may have tagged along with your friends. The Ouija Board isn't evil in itself—although there can be attachments on them—it's the intention of its use, and the door that intention opens, that can be problematic.

The Demon at the Inn.

Ouija Boards are not allowed at the Cashtown Inn, the headquarters for Lee and Longstreet the first day of the Battle of Gettysburg. I'm quite fond of the Confederate soldiers there, and I have spent much time talking with them about their lives and travels. I am also protective of them and don't want demonic entities around.

Patty Wilson and I arrived for an event we were holding over the weekend. Jack, the owner, asked us to check out one of the guest rooms. He had a complaint the previous night about something rattling the window and making noise.

We headed up the stairs, with a box of salt and our friend Carol Nesbitt in tow. I could feel the energy of an entity move around the room in circles. We asked the spirit of a soldier what had happened there, and he explained that guests had used a Ouija Board and called a spirit from the Bible by name. Guess what? He came.

Patty began the cleanse, "I demand all destructive entities leave this person, place, and property, in the name of the Father, Son, and Holy Spirit." Over and over she calmly repeated the phrase while she threw sea salt around the perimeter of the room.

I prayed the Lord's Prayer and recited Psalms 23 and 100. We had to keep going, and Patty suggested we sing. The only song I could think of was *Jesus Loves Me*.

Carol and I sang over and over, "Jesus loves me this I know, for the Bible tells me so, little ones to Him belong, they are weak but He is strong." *One hundred Bottles of Beer on the Wall* could have been sung faster. At last, the little creature was gone, and the room was quiet again.

A few years ago, a friend of mine went to a party and taped a reputable psychic using an Ouija Board. The psychic told everyone it was safe for her to use because she could discern between different entities. When my friend played back the tape, there was EVP of an entity saying the psychic did not know he was there. You can always shut the door, but when others are around constantly opening new ones, you do not have control over what enters. Where there is the intention to talk to random entities through devices such as a Ouija Board, spirit box, ovilus, or even via spirit photography such as Instrumental Transcommunication (ITC), a door can be created that must be shut.

Electronic Voice Phenomena (EVP)

Electronic voice phenomena (EVP) is created when sound frequencies that are inaudible to the human ear are caught on tape, such as spirit voices. Sarah Estep was the premier pioneer researcher in EVP in the United States, and she was considered one of the world's leading experts in the field.[11]

I have taped close to a thousand EVPs, and I find that while I have tape recorders that work especially well, taping with a regular tape recorder works also, if you add white noise such as a fan, or if you tape outdoors. Anyone can record EVP. In fact, the outgoing message on my mother's answering machine even captured a ghost saying "thank you." Capturing EVP has more to do with the equipment than the person

---

[11] https://atransc.org/sarah-estep-memorial/

holding the equipment. However, if spirits like you, they are more likely to want to chat. Also, spirits will pull energy off of people so they can have the strength to talk, thus the more well rested you are, the better your EVP may be. You can also carry batteries in your pocket, so the batteries will be drained before you are. Sensitive people know where spirits are, and I think for this reason, we may get more EVP. And, I think it is easier to draw energy from sensitive and outgoing people.

However, be careful at home. The more frequently you talk with spirits, no matter the device—the more active they will become. And, others will follow. When more come, you'll feel more, hear more, and see more. Don't treat your home as a venue for your personal paranormal investigations, unless you like hearing and seeing them. In that case, you probably would not be reading this guide. And even if you do, I promise, it can get out of hand quickly. No one knows better than I do. I've had it happen to me, and I've seen it happen to hundreds of others, as well. No one is exempt.

The Demon at the Farm.
In April of 2017, my friend Stef welcomed popular television personalities to tape a

paranormal show at her farm, the David Stewart Farm in Gettysburg. It was once a Civil War field hospital and has a number of ghosts from native tribes to settlers and soldiers. When she heard the group was investigating without anyone sensitive, she was concerned. And rightfully so; our homes are our sanctuaries. Someone should be on the scene who knows what is happening spiritually and can handle the situation if things take a turn for the worse.

Television networks continue to air shows modeled after shows that have been popular in the past. They continue to buy similar paranormal shows because it's a model that works for viewership—and thus, revenue. I don't condemn this practice; I understand—I use to direct marketing at a national cable television network. However, this revenue model for paranormal investigations doesn't always include having mediums who are either on the show or available to help off camera, and this is a mistake. I was glad Stef asked me to be available in case things went bad. And they did, quickly.

The actors were in the bedrooms that were once operating rooms, or "amputation rooms." Remember when I said never to ask for any random entity? Here comes the cautionary tale. During their break from filming, I walked upstairs to get a feel for the energy, for my friend's safety.

As I climbed the stairs and stood on the landing in front of one of the bedrooms, I was attacked by a mist that choked me and I couldn't breathe. I ran down the stairs and out the front door so I could take a breath and figure out what to do with this low-level demonic entity. But it followed me and wouldn't let me re-enter. I told it to leave. I prayed. It taunted me and called me names. I gave it fair warning that it could leave on its own right then, or I would make it leave. I have read demons are smart, but I've yet to meet one that left when I asked. It came forward through the front door at me, and I showed no mercy. I called on God's help–loudly I may add–and in a few minutes it was carried away by angels.

I walked to the side of the house where the film crew and actors were standing, after having listened to me fight the entity. As I approached, a hush fell on the group, and they walked away. I sensed they were not sensitive and not only didn't believe me, but didn't truly understand how dangerous their actions were and could have been, if I had not stepped in.

When the show aired, it was apparent that I had given them an idea. They taped in the basement of a shop in town and said it was the David Stewart Farm. They played what they claimed was EVP that said "demon," and they concluded the farm had a demon when they arrived. As a result, I received messages from worried folks who didn't want to investigate there. I explained that they were not even at the farm at the time, which was evident in the video.

Fortunately, I have worked with some of the best and most experienced producers in the industry, and this has not been the case on any shows where I have appeared. And this year, I have begun to consult with production companies both before and throughout the filming. I usually remote view the location and draw a picture of the area before I know where it is. I'll identify active areas, names of ghosts to speak with, and where and when the actors could be affected adversely. I teach the producers, crew, and actors how to protect themselves. I am hoping that using a medium for these shows will become the standard and not the exception.

But in any case, if you want to talk to a loved one with your tape recorder, at least walk out of your house, or do it somewhere else–if you believe you have a problematic haunting.

Pendulums and Dowsing Rods

Pendulums and dowsing rods are great tools to talk to the dead when on a ghost investigation, or at an historic site. However, do not use them at home to talk with any spirits if you have had trouble there. Pendulums and dowsing rods are different than Ouija Boards because they are used in a one-on-one conversation with spirits. Although risks are minimized, they still can open a door just as Ouija Boards do.

It doesn't matter if you are recording EVP or using a pendulum or dowsing rod, if you are talking to spirits, it is important to know with whom you are speaking. You can specify that you will only talk with spirits of love and light, or, you may want to specify a human spirit, such as "the woman of the house," or "the highest ranking Union officer." If you don't specify, other entities may come in, and you'll find yourself reading this guide again.

Always be sure to say a prayer of protection beforehand, and pay attention to how a spirit feels. When you want to speak to someone in particular, ask yes or no questions to confirm the spirit's identity. And, in the case of loved ones, know the answers, before you ask. Negative spirits can never feel good or make you feel love. When the mood or vibration of the energy changes, I find out who it is, or I stop talking altogether.

While you won't be doing this at home, you don't want to talk to something or someone who would follow you home. When you leave, tell spirits not to follow you. And, say another prayer for your safety, and for the spirits. While they still may follow you, this often helps.

If your pendulum begins to shake or vibrate without moving in the predetermined "yes" or "no" direction, another spirit may be pushing its way in. Stop, pray, and try again later. Spirits are excited to talk and many times, they all want the opportunity to do so.

If you ever feel a sudden headache or pressure while using a pendulum, stop immediately and say a prayer, and discontinue using it for a while. A headache and pressure could be the sign of a malevolent entity. I've encountered human spirits who were not nice people, and they have negative entities attached to them. So don't think that simply asking for a human is going to keep you safe; you also have to feel what is going on around you.

Don't think that just because you pray, you are protected from all negative energy. God protects us when we ask and believe, but sometimes that protection is simply common sense. If it doesn't feel right, then by all means, stop. We've all heard the story of the man who sat on his rooftop during a flood and three boats came by to save him. He tells each that he prayed and God will save him, and then he sends the boats on their way. If you run into a building to seek entities on a paranormal investigation, or if you're just plain stupid and don't get on the boat, you're probably going to need more help than a quick prayer of protection.

Be sure to cleanse your pendulum. There are different ways, but I'm impatient, so I hold it under a running faucet for a couple of minutes while I pray for its cleansing. It works!

I have talked to negative entities with a pendulum before, by mistake. Spirits may lie about their identity, just as people do. I command them to tell the truth in the name of the Trinity three times. If they are not who they say they are, they usually fess up on round three. However, if I stop to feel the nature of the energy and it doesn't feel loving, or if I get a headache, I back away and stop talking.

I get more energy attachments when I use a pendulum because the energy touches me to move the device. I never let my children use pendulums, but now that they are older, I suggest they use dowsing rods[12] so the spirit does not touch them.

Dowsing rods have many uses. They are used to find water, talk to spirits, and find graves. Cemeteries typically bury people east to west, and the rods will cross over a person's feet and straighten over the head and torso. I usually use a pendulum or nothing at all, since dowsing rods use a spirit's energy too quickly,

---

[12] http://theothersidetv.ca/ghost-hunting-resources/ghost-hunting-tips-tricks/dowsing-rods-investigation/

and I'm quite loquacious. And since I hear them, it's easier to confirm answers quickly with a pendulum. Many times there are multiple spirits talking, and then I'll use a pendulum so I can feel its energy and differentiate its voice from the others.

The Visit at the James Gettys Hotel.

On one of my investigative weekends at the James Gettys Hotel in Gettysburg, I showed a group how to feel spirit energy and use a pendulum safely. We investigated the hotel, and later a woman in my group excitedly shared her story. She revealed, "I met General Longstreet!"

I asked further questions to find out that she had asked to speak to a human, a Confederate. A ghost came and started moving her pendulum. She asked yes or no questions and he answered that he was a general. The first general she could think of was Longstreet. She asked, "Are you General Longstreet?" The ghost moved the pendulum in the direction she had instructed for "yes."

She was absolutely certain she was talking to General Longstreet. There are a lot of things I've learned since doing this work, and I have met folks I've never imagined meeting. However, I don't think General Longstreet would be hanging out in a bathroom at the James Gettys Hotel.

Lots of ghosts think it is fun to play around. Be sure you know the answers to questions before you ask. Even if you don't know the states, companies, and militia that a general oversees, those are questions you can ask and verify later. It always helps to take along a sense of humor, too. When I went to meet "General Longstreet," I found him to be a very amusing prankster named Sam.

Inviting Spirits

I regularly see paranormal shows where people call on "ghosts" and "demons" or "something" or "whoever is here" to touch them, manifest, throw something, or cause physical activity. There is not a word in my vocabulary to describe this depth of stupid.

Then, these people are surprised when they receive burning scratches or things fly around the room and doors slam. If they had more sense they would know it doesn't end there.

These entities can cause aches and pains when they attach, and they will also follow them home, even if they tell them not to do so. We're talking a whole new genre of ignorance here, folks. Don't try it.

I realize that I have the benefit of being psychic, but for those who are not, asking for a human is a good starting place. Even as a medium, I've had negative entities block me from hearing my guides. These negative entities are usually louder and easier to hear, but you will never feel love from them. Feeling is more important than seeing or hearing because the bad can pretend to be good, but they can never make you feel goodness or love. Pay attention to how a location makes you feel.

The Subjugated Biker.
He rode a Harley and seemed to be a nice guy, but he had traded his soul to the devil and was paying the price. I never knew this spirit's name, but I saw him drive his motorcycle into the dining room of the Cashtown Inn, look me in the eye and exclaim, "Help me please!"

My team was hosting an event at the time. Our historian was lecturing, and I leaned over to Patty Wilson and whispered, "Is there any possibility that you sense a dude on a motorcycle with demons swirling around him, to your left? Or, am I sleep deprived?"

Patty focused for a minute and then looked at me and said, "Let's go in the lobby to handle this one."

When we went into the lobby, the spirit told us that when he was alive, he promised the devil his soul in exchange for things of this world. He didn't believe Satan was real, and he did not know the serious nature of his action. He went on to explain that since he died, he had been tormented and attacked by demons, who surrounded him and wouldn't leave him alone. He was exhausted and didn't know where to turn, and another spirit told him to come see us. There is a network of spirits on the other side, and it's not the first time spirits have visited the Cashtown Inn and waited for Patty or me to arrive and help them.

This was certainly a conundrum for us. We had in our midst, a soul who desperately wanted to go to Heaven instead of Hell, and a room of demonic entities who were attacking him. They resembled swarming bees around this weary man. The situation seemed a little far-fetched, even for me. We had to figure out what to do–fast. So, we called in help.

While Patty prayed aloud, I listened and focused on what was going on around us. Soon, I heard a man say he had come to help. I interrupted Patty's prayer and said, "A priest is here now. He says his name is Malachi Martin." Patty's eyes grew large. "Who did you say?"

I confirmed, "Malachi Martin."

Partly incredulous and partly excited, Patty replied, "Malachi Martin? You know who that is right?"

"I have no clue. Should I?" I replied.

Patty said, "He's a very well known priest; an exorcist."

I was excited we had received the spiritual gift of Father Martin, simply by asking.

While Father Martin dealt with the demonic entities present, we told the spirit of the motorcyclist to denounce Satan and his minions right then, and pledge himself to Jesus Christ. He did so, and we asked God to open the door to Heaven and take him home. He cried from relief and happiness, thanked us, and then crossed over with angels at this side.

This wasn't the last time I called on Father Martin.

Inciting Spirits

Don't be a bully. I feel that bears repeating— do not taunt entities. Many do it on television, but this is a very serious mistake. Don't do it.

Pride and Prejudice.
Several years ago a good friend of mine enlisted my help for his friend. He lived in North Carolina, and since I live in Maryland, I instructed him over the phone. I told the man what he needed to do, as I have explained in this guide. I reiterated that he should not talk to the entity, nor tell it that he was going to get rid of it. Something exceptionally evil had taken

residence in this man's home, and it began to manifest regularly. He needed to be careful. We talked until his confidence soared and he felt comfortable he could do what was needed to remove the entity.

After our call, I couldn't get in touch with him for days, and our mutual friend told me he was in a car accident. Apparently, after he got off the phone with me, he confronted the entity and told him he was going to "kick his ass." Then he laughed at it and told it he wasn't scared and it couldn't hurt him. He got in his car to go to the store to get some sea salt, and he was in a horrific accident. He was in the hospital for months before he moved away. I never heard from him again. The home remains vacant, over a decade later.

The lesson here is that while this is a battle of wills, do not let pride be a part of it. Just follow my guidelines prayerfully and remember your goal is to cleanse negative energy and that your battle should not be a prideful one.

The Good Fight.

When we go out of our way to mess with Satan and the demonic realm, there are consequences. When we stay in our own space and pray, we are protected, but whether we desire to walk with Satan, or combat Satan, there are repercussions. I knew this when I was asked to be on *Ghost Brothers: Haunted Houseguests*. I remote viewed Lori's home, and I felt comfortable that I could help. And, Lori desperately needed help.

However, by cleansing her house, I was now on Lucifer's radar. Fighting the entities that weekend was nothing compared to the attack on me that ensued after I left. While Lori and her family were better, my hotel room was cold and had changed. The crew had attachments that I either removed or prayed over. A nasty entity followed behind me, and I spent an hour in the airport praying it away. Two more were in my suitcase attached to the clothing I wore that night. And for about six weeks, energy would dive-bomb me around the clock, waking me up, distracting me, and giving me headaches.

When I told my friend, Demonologist Dave Juliano, he said, "You know *that* was the attack don't you?" And yes, I did. It finally went away and life went back to normal until the show aired. Within the same week, two friends who are mediums called to say they had dreams about me. They warned me to be careful because Satan was after me and planned to hurt me. I could only laugh. If Satan could get to me, he would have already. I don't scare easily. I pray and am protected. That's why he has to go into the dreams of others.

While revising this book, my endnotes disappeared and my stove caught on fire. It was probably a coincidence, but I heard one entity take credit. Like ISIS, these creatures will take credit when no credit is due, but hearing one sent me into action. I had forgotten to pray for a couple of days, and while this does not open the door to demonic entities for typical people, that's not the case for me. Not only am I "on the radar" for standing up against evil in the past, but I am the midst of writing a book about it, while writing this guide on how to cleanse it. I'm not the most hated person by those in Hell, but every time I receive a threat, I know I'm doing something right.

I asked my guide to explain the details of what was going on around me that I couldn't see. He told me to cleanse immediately and once again, I called in Father Martin. I was rundown and allergies had led to a sinus infection and earache. I asked Father Martin if he would intercede on my behalf and do whatever was necessary to exorcise my house while I went to bed and slept for a couple days. Graciously, he agreed, and a two days later he told me he was done. He warned me, "lock your doors." I figured this was a metaphor, but I'll hedge my bets and lock my house too. He also told me not to let a day go by that I don't thank God and pray for protection for myself and my family. We will all be protected, that is, until I go into battle again and need to call reinforcements.

6.

THE CLEANSING

By this point, you should have walked around your home to see what you feel. If you are cleansing your home because you have an active haunting, you should also have talked aloud to ask spirits to leave you alone. Your home is a place of immunity where you can be yourself, and you don't want to be bothered there.

Preparation

In preparation for the cleansing, you should be well rested. I cannot stress this enough. You may become exhausted doing this, depending on what you encounter. Working with spirits takes a lot of energy. Whether you realize you are expending energy or not, you are. Spirits use energy to communicate, manifest, and exist in this realm. Whether they hang out near a fuse box, a water source, or you, they are drawing energy to exist. Don't be surprised if you are very tired after the cleansing.

You'll need:
• A supportive friend;

- Sea salt (optional—holy water or oil); and
- Prayers, hymns, Bible or prayer book such as *Armor of God* by Dave Juliano.

The Supportive Friend.

Supportive friends are ones that stick it out through thick or thin, and this could be one of those times. Your support person can help you feel when the room is lighter, happier, or has a different emotion. And, you'll have someone to help if you need it.

I was very glad to have support at the Tillie Pierce House in Gettysburg. I walked into the blue room and right back out, as I could barely breathe. The owners of the inn explained they had a few "runners" from that room, or in other words, guests who literally ran out of the inn in the middle of the night, never to return.

As I investigated the situation, I found the ghost of a soldier who was not in his right mind and did not realize he was dead. He was a Union soldier behind Confederate lines, and he was scared he would be caught. When he heard my Southern accent, he roared at me to "GET OUT!" Then he disappeared. I discovered he was going directly upstairs into the attic and hiding under the rafters. I couldn't reason with him, and I did not sleep in that room.

The next night, a group of paranormal investigators came to film, and they asked me to help. I was having an event next door, so during a break, I stopped by the Tillie Pierce House with another investigator. I went into the attic, and the nasty spirit was once again hiding under the rafters, and he wouldn't leave. He screamed at me to leave him alone, so I did not approach him, but I explained that I was there to help him.

Feeling his relief, I shifted my weight onto my left foot. The board was not nailed down and as my ankle turned, I fell straight down through the attic floor and into the room below. I looked like a wishbone as one foot was stuck above my head in the attic, and the other foot was hanging below the ceiling, well into the blue room below. The other investigator stood at a sturdy six feet, three inches, and he reached down, scooped me up, and pulled me back into the attic. His strength was the paranormal feat in this story. The entire embarrassing moment was caught on film, much to my chagrin. So, another person is always helpful, if only for safety–or rescue!

Sea Salt, Holy Water or Holy Oil.
You may want some sea salt, or some people use sage. Holy water or oil is an added bonus. I have always believed that these were used as metaphors and it was the prayers that worked. However recently, I was told by guides to put rock salt around the house and that each of these things (salt, holy water, oil and sage), have a positive vibration and effect.

I never use sage because I am very allergic to it, and I always use sea salt. I have holy water, and I will use it to mark doors and entrances when I encounter a demonic entity, or feel it could be beneficial.

How to Make Holy Water and Holy Oil:
Usually, holy water is water that has been blessed by a member of the clergy. However, as a Protestant, I believe that Christ is in us (Romans 8:10), and we do not have to go through a priest to ask for forgiveness, or to make holy water. I hold the water in my hand, pray over it and ask God to bless it in the

name of God the Father, God the Son, and the Holy Spirit.

However, Keisha Matlock-Glass, Associate Minister of Missionary Baptist Church tells me that she buys water and places it on a Bible, open to Psalm 91, and leaves it for seven days. Because my Bible is on my Kindle, she told me I could use a printout of Psalm 91. (In case you don't have a Bible handy, or if can't spare your Bible for a week, see Chaper 9.)

Reverend Matlock-Glass also says she uses the same method for holy oil. She uses 100 percent extra virgin olive oil, and places it on Psalm 91 for a week. When doing a cleansing, she buys David's Kosher Sea Salt. I've prayed with this lovely woman; I take her word on this! However, if you're Catholic and don't have a priest handy, you can also purchase a small bottle for less than $10 on Amazon.

The size of your house and your property will determine how much sea salt you will need, but for a three bedroom house on a half acre, you may want to put about 1/4 to a half cup of sea salt in a small open container to use. If you have a farm with a lot of acreage, you'll need more, of course. You will want to make sure all of your property is cleansed.

Prayers, Hymns and Such.

Some people use the Bible, which is always a good source. I also use the book *Armor of God* by Dave Juliano. *Armor of God* is a compilation of many prayers, used by a variety of Christian belief systems, to protect oneself and others from negative entities or evil spirits. There are also pagan prayers and prayers to the goddess included. There are prayers for personal protection and the protection of others, as well as prayers for spiritual welfare, exorcism and deliverance. You may want the book as a resource whether you are asking for protection as you sleep, or as an aid for spiritual assistance.

The Cleanse

Step 1: *Pray for Protection*

Before you begin, say a prayer of protection. Ask God to protect you, and that His angels may shield you and those with you from any negative energy during the process. I have included a prayer in Chapter 9, that you may wish to use.

You can also visualize a bubble of white light around you. Envision white light entering through the top of your head, and as you breathe out, fill the bubble with light. When the bubble is full, you are done, but you'll need to keep this up every couple of hours.

This is where the book of prayers also comes in. I suggest you say a hedge prayer for protection of the home, such as the one I have included in Chapter 9. Or you may want to use another hedge prayer suiting your personal beliefs or religion.

Step 2: *Cleanse*

With a container of sea salt, go to the bottom floor of the home, whether this is a basement or first floor. You do not need to go into a crawl space under your home. You will go room by room, and in each room, you will walk the perimeter and sprinkle a tiny amount of salt along each wall and in the corners. While sprinkling salt, say in an assertive voice, "I command all destructive entities leave this person, this place, and this property, in the name of the Father, the Son, and the Holy Spirit." (However, if you pray to Yahweh, Allah, or Spirit, this is the time.)

Once you say this, begin saying it again. You will say it hundreds of times, by the end of the cleansing. Be sure to say it as I have because if there are negative entities, you don't want to play a game of semantics with them. Ordering them off the people, place, and the property makes it clear you want them gone from everyone and everything. Continue from room to room, and don't forget the closets. You don't want anything negative to hide. Sprinkle salt behind dressers and around the perimeter of the closets and utility rooms.

If the crawl space is under the house, during Step 5, I usually envision white light and pray for angels to cleanse the space for me. However, if the space is in the attic under rafters or in an unfinished portion that is hard to reach, you will want to envision white light and say a prayer at the time you cleanse that floor of your home. Ask for angels to cleanse the space that is impossible for you to reach, and to block any entrances so nothing may enter your living space.

Step 3: Pray.

When you have finished with each room, say a prayer. If there had been anything negative there, the room should now feel lighter. If it doesn't, keep praying until it does. If I encounter a particularly stubborn entity, or a spot that may feel heavy, I'll pray there longer.

When you have cleansed all the rooms on that floor, say a hedge prayer, and/or pray the Lord's prayer, or other prayers. I also make the sign of the cross with my hand, above windows and doors and pray nothing negative will enter through those passages. If you have holy water, you can use it now. How long you pray will depend on how it feels. It could take a minute or a half hour.

Step 4: *Lather, Rinse, Repeat.*

After Step 3, Go to the next higher floor and repeat the steps, and so on, until the entire house is cleansed from inside.

Step 5: *Cleanse along your home's foundation.*

Walk outside and do the same procedure around the perimeter of the house. Sprinkle sea salt and say the same prayer: "I command all destructive entities to leave this person, this place, and this property, in the name of the Father, Son, and Holy Spirit."

Step 6: *Cleanse along your property line.*

Once the perimeter of your house has been cleansed, walk around the perimeter of your property. If you own a large property with outbuildings, cleanse those as you would a house. If there are any spots that feel odd, be sure to say the cleansing prayer, and then say the Lord's prayer, or other prayers and scripture, until it feels lighter and you know any residual energy or entities have gone.

Pray and ask God to put angels at the corners of the property to keep everyone within safe. I also pray every night that angels stand at the four corners of my bed to protect me, and my family. You may want to do the same.

Remember, these are spiritual prayers and God will make sure that unwanted spirits do not set foot on the property. So, please don't be mad at me if your mother-in-law continues to drop in unexpectedly.

Step 7: *Cleanse your car.*
Cars should be cleansed too; energy and spirits can hop in your car or follow it home. After hosting a paranormal weekend in Gettysburg, I was so exhausted I could no

longer feel much of anything. I walked in my back door and my daughter said, "Mom, you brought home four soldiers. You have to be more careful!" I had forgotten to pray.

A few months ago, my friend Linda used this guide to cleanse her home. It worked well. However, when her "supportive friend" returned to visit, the negative spirit returned with her. The malevolent entity had been expelled from Linda's house and caught a ride home with her friend, and then hitched a ride back. The second cleansing did the trick; we had him carried away to another dimension.

I also mentioned that negative entities left Lori's house when filming, but when the production crew crossed the property line to drive home, some of the entities must have hopped in their cars. I was the last to arrive at the hotel, and I continued to cleanse and pray them away.

Now I pray whenever I get in my car. I typically say, "Dear Lord, I ask you to cleanse this car. I plead the blood of Jesus Christ over this car and over all within. I also ask you to keep me safe in my travels, and please do not let any entities, negative energy or ghosts, enter the car along the way. In the name of the Father, the Son, and the Holy Spirit I pray."

During the Cleanse

When doing the cleanse, do not do anything else until you are done. Do not stop for lunch. Do not take a phone call. Do not pass "GO." Just concentrate on the cleanse.

What if bad energy just won't go?

1. *Pray*. If you feel that you need extra time in an area, or if there is something that still will not leave, just stop anywhere you feel is necessary and let your senses be your guide—say prayers and ask God to send white light and angels. I say the Lord's Prayer and I recite psalms that I memorized as a child. I have also been known to sing the children's song, *Jesus Loves Me,* when I can think of nothing else to say, or I've exhausted all the prayers I know. Eventually, the most stubborn entities will figure out they are wasting their time, and you are more stubborn than they are. And, they leave. After all, this is a battle of wills.

2. *Be assertive!* Stand your ground. Be a mama bear. Tell anything negative that it is your

house and they do not have the right to be there. You don't have to yell to command respect. I may yell if I know what I'm up against and my guides direct me to do so. However, it is effective to raise your voice to pray, and call on Archangel Michael to fight the battle for you.

3. *Use your senses.* Do not taunt the negative entity, and do not try to hold a two-way conversation. In this situation, without the aide of a medium, use your senses. You do not need to know what is there to get rid of it. Do not try to use a pendulum to find out more, by any means, and do not try to get EVP. Just tell it to leave, and call on God for help. Do not engage the spirit.

4. *Get Help By Proxy. Don't hesitate to call in help from the other side. Help can come from angels, saints, and even from deceased exorcists or ministers.*

Help by Proxy.

Recently, another medium told me that her son bought an ambulance and converted it into a camper that he keeps on his farm. She told him not to do it, but he didn't listen. "Now," she told me, "he has a very dark energy on his property."

I suggested she pray for a priest who had been an exorcist, to intercede on her behalf and get rid of the negative entity. A few days later I received the message: "Last Sunday I did my long distance clearing and used your suggestion of calling on the spirit of a priest who was an exorcist. It TOTALLY worked!" She went on to say that her son and daughter are empaths and they are constantly drawing energy to their property, unknowingly.

Calling on help from the other side does not need to be limited to angels. We get the spiritual help we ask for, so if you didn't know before, you can call on clergy, as well.

After the Cleanse

Even if you cleansed your home as a cautionary measure, it probably feels a little better—even lighter—after the cleanse. But what if you had a difficult haunting before the cleanse? Your job has just begun.

Cleanse Again.

In the case of a problematic haunting, you'll always have to be on guard—and even fight. It's just like having cancer. If you continue to do the work, you will stay in remission. But, any disturbance can change the dynamic. When this happens, don't think twice. Don't let yourself have the opportunity to fear; cleanse and take control. Fast action will prevent anything from gaining a stronghold.

In very bad cases, I tell people to cleanse every day for a month, then every week for several months, and then every month. Typically, a second cleanse the next week doesn't hurt. You may want to cleanse every month, especially if you have lots of people coming and going, or there is drug use and alcohol. Or, something has caused people to be sad, angry, or in pain.

I don't do formal cleanses on a set schedule in my house, although I continue to do them. We are a sensitive family and energy follows us home and comes into our space fairly often. When it does, one of us notices and we figure out who or what it is, and if it's new, it has to leave. Sometimes I pray, talk to it, or have it dragged away. It all depends on its nature.

Cross Over Ghosts.

There are spirits in my home who do not want to cross over into Heaven because everyone they know is still here. Despite my explanation that they can still return, they tell me they are already here, and so there is no point in taking the chance. I have become friends with spirits of many of the enslaved people on the grounds of the plantation where I live. They have looked after my kids growing up, and I feel they are family. So, it's important I clearly state that those who lived on the plantation may stay; I am not ordering them to leave their home.

From time to time I'll cleanse a property, and the ghosts will want to cross over, either as a result of persuasion, or because they didn't know how to do so on their own. In this case, I may cross over some before I start the cleanse, and during the cleanse I'll tell more ghosts I encounter to meet me outside afterwards and I'll help them crossover too. See Chapter 7 for the "how to" description to cross over ghosts.

Cleanse the Cleanse.

When should I vacuum? Personally, I use so little salt that I don't vacuum it unless I'm cleaning the room anyway. However, I typically suggest to leave it down a week.

Maintenance.

Don't forget you have to maintain a home that is free from unwanted energy. See Chapter 8 for suggestions.

7.

CROSSING OVER GHOSTS

When we help spirits cross over, we can't make them go. It is their own decision. However, we can help them by interceding on their behalf.

If you're sensitive and you see or feel what is going on, it makes the ritual of crossing over ghosts easier, however, if you are not sensitive, you can accomplish the same, with these prayers, this ritual, and faith. I have no doubt there are many ways to cross over spirits in various religions. I have an angel who is always with me when I go on investigations and cross over ghosts. He tells me what is going on every step of the way. It is difficult for me to focus on feeling love, saying prayers, and sensing spirits, all at the same time. My angel helps me through this process and taught me how to do what I am about to tell you. You may also want to pray for help before you begin, and an angel will come to you, if only you ask.

My prayers and instructions are written below in six easy steps, followed by more explanation. If this is your first time, you may want to read through the process and then highlight the prayers and wording I use. That way, you'll be able to see exactly what I recommend when you are in the midst of helping the spirits to go back home.

Once when cleansing my own house, I heard crying in my daughter's closet. When I went upstairs, I realized that the ghost of a little girl was afraid that I was trying to make her leave. Since she was only six when she died, her child-like mind was without the ability to understand my intention. I explained to her I meant for "destructive" entities to leave, and that meant "bad stuff," and she was a good little girl. She was relieved, and I learned to be sure and explain what I am going to do before I begin. Not all spirits are in the same frame of mind as we are.

I begin my cleanse by saying aloud something like, "If there are loving spirits here who once lived in a body on earth, I don't want to frighten you, especially if you have children or are a child. I am going to do a cleansing in the house to get rid of all the negative spirits who bother us here. At the end, please meet me in the kitchen, and I am happy to ask your loved ones to come and I can help you go home to Heaven to be with those you love. Please be mindful of any children and explain to them what is going on, so I won't scare them if they think I want them to leave." I also don't give ghosts much notice because I don't want to announce aloud to anything negative that I am going to come after it, until I do.

After the cleanse, I meet ghosts in a pre-determined location, and I cross them over. This means I help them move on to the other dimension or plane that we commonly call Heaven. You can do the same by following the instructions below.

Step 1: *Let the spirits know that you are there to help them cross over into Heaven.*

I always tell them it is time for me to help them go to Heaven, and if they know anyone else who would like to go, please go find them and return. I usually wait until they tell me they are back, but you could set a time, like "in 15 minutes." If you do this before the cleanse, let them know you will help after the cleanse, and that gives them time to prepare and round up others.

Step 2: *Explain that God will accept them.*

When I am ready to begin, I explain that if they think God won't take them into Heaven, they are wrong. God is a god of love, not hellfire and damnation. Despite what they may have heard in their church services long ago, or what may have occurred on a battlefield or in their life, God is forgiving and loving, and the path to Heaven awaits them, if they decide to go. I also explain that they can always come back to visit loved ones still here.

I explain this because sometimes spirits who don't think they want to go, or are unsure, watch other spirits to see what happens. If I proactively offer this explanation, there is a chance they will cross over, and not wait to make that decision until after I have left a location.

Step 3: *Begin the ritual. You can say your own words, or use the following:*
"Everyone that is here, now is the time to begin. I want you to focus on love. I want you

to feel love in your heart. You may want to think about your mother or father, husband or wife, girlfriend or boyfriend. You may want to think about your children, your horse or your dog. It's important to feel love–and concentrate on that love–because love opens the door into Heaven."

You will want to focus on love too, and wait until you feel love and happiness in your heart. Then continue.

Step 4: *Pray.*

"Dear Lord, I ask you please to open the door into Heaven. Please hold it open and let these precious souls see the white light and feel your love.

It is time for them to go home to you. Please send your angels and their loved ones to come for them. Whether that be a mother or father, relative, spouse, or a minister or priest, please send someone to help each person."

At this time I usually see mothers come from Heaven to greet their children, among other relatives, friends, spouses, ministers, and even pets. Everyone is happy and many are crying.

I start to feel the energy change as they move on to Heaven.

Step 5: *Tell them to go.*

By now, you may feel that these souls have already crossed over. However, for anyone left or still crying and hugging their mama, I say:

"It's time to go. Go through the light and to God. It's time. Your loved ones are here, as well as angels."

On occasion, I hear someone panic and call out to me if they cannot see anyone there for them. Sometimes there are loved ones present that they can't see, and at times, I do not sense anyone. In this case, I may add:

"Dear Lord please send angels to help this (these) soul(s), and escort her/him (them) back home to you. Also, please do whatever needs to be done energetically so that this soul can see who you have sent, so he (or she) may go back home to you. Some have been hurt, and some may not be themselves. I ask that you help them to see the angels and their loved ones. I ask that these angels act on their behalf now and do whatever is necessary to help the souls who wish to cross over, finally go home."

I may also add:
"See the white light. It's there. Go in the direction of the light and step into it."

Sometimes ghosts think I'm tricking them or they don't believe me, and they won't go. That's a commentary on their life and why they may be here in the first place. If they won't go, you can't make them. It's their decision. You can pray for them later and for angels to try again on your behalf.

All Dogs Go to Heaven.
When my twins were young, I took them to Westover Plantation, between Richmond and Williamsburg, Virginia. I met Elizabeth, the spirit of a young girl, whom I never would have met if she had not sought to play with my daughter, Annie. I couldn't get the child to cross over, but she was there without any of her family. Perhaps her family watched over her from the other side, but she was unable to see them. Being a mother myself, I was determined to help this child.

I prayed for a few minutes, and no one she recognized came for her from Heaven. She stomped her foot and refused to go. I prayed again and again and she had her mind set; she was staying. Finally, I saw a big brown dog jump out of the light, and she screamed happily and hugged him, and disappeared into the light without a second thought.

Step 6: *One last prayer.*

You should feel the room is lighter. At this time, I like to bestow a blessing on these souls as they go home. I have always been fond of Aaron's Blessing (Numbers 6:23 - 27):

"'May The Lord bless you and keep you; May the Lord make his face to shine upon you and be gracious to you; May the Lord lift up his countenance upon you and give you peace.' I ask this in the name of the Father, the Son, and the Holy Spirit. Amen."

Then, I pray silently and thank God and the angels for helping these souls. And, for letting me help facilitate their trip home.

8.

MAINTENANCE

After the cleansing, there are things that can be done to make sure the house is light and feels good, especially if there was cause to cleanse the house originally.

Don't argue.
While this may be second nature to many people, I find it is incredibly difficult when raising children. When I was pregnant with twins, I complained to my doctor. He told me, "Let this be your first lesson that you will never be able to control anything that your children do. It's only the beginning." No prophet has ever been more wise.

When arguments happen, I silently pray and ask for angels to come and change the vibration to make it a happy home.

Play music.
Music often inspires us and changes our mood and feelings. Listening to Bach's *Orchestral*

Suite No. 3 in D will give you a very different feeling than Pearl Jam's *Even Flow*. Music is a good way to change how your home feels. I suggest you play music that inspires and makes you happy.

My favorite "go to" music for this purpose is by Hildegard Von Bingen.[13] Hildegard was born around the year 1098, and she began having visions as a child. Today, we would call her a psychic medium, but because she was Catholic in the Middle Ages, she is called "spiritually aware." She became a nun and wrote angelically-inspired music, in praise of God. Her music is widely available and can be found on Youtube.[14]

Do not watch violent movies or television shows.

Why would not watching Dexter have anything to do with the vibration in a home? Thoughts are things. Remember when I mentioned positive energy attracts positive energy, and negative energy attracts negative energy? After your home is cleansed, you want to keep

---

[13] https://en.wikipedia.org/wiki/Hildegard_of_Bingen

[14] https://www.youtube.com/watch?v=v6qFCYRQKVA

it balanced. You do not want to create fear, be scared, or exhibit negative emotions.

Recently, I began researching dark entities, and in doing so, I have watched videos and television shows about them. My thoughts attracted a negative entity that I prayed away. I asked my friend Rosemary Ellen Guiley about her encounters with anything negative also. She told me that when researching the *Encyclopedia of Demons and Demonology,* she would write long hours late at night, and at times, she felt something negative visited as well.

You may have heard people say not to repeat the names of demons aloud. Our thoughts are energetic vibrations, just like music. And as such, they are broadcast and recognized by other energies. Negative entities are going to be repelled by love, but attracted by negative emotions—or even thoughts while researching or writing about them.

Be positive.
Live happily and prayerfully. Think good thoughts and continue to pray to your supreme higher power. Each day I say a prayer of thanks and then I continue with prayers of

protection for my family. Each night, I ask God for angels to stand guard around the beds of my children. And when I pray, my children sleep at peace from other-worldly interference.

9.

PRAYERS

Prayer is highly underrated. When I cleansed Lori's home after we filmed, I passed her dresser and felt energy. When I stopped to remove it, I perceived a woman, so I did nothing more. I had much to do in little time, and I picked my battles.

A few weeks after I had been home, I awoke at 3 a.m., with Lori on my mind. I prayed for her safe keeping. Then, I prayed that angels would take away anything malevolent in her home, and I went back to sleep and forgot all about it.

Lori contacted me for the first time after the show aired, six months after the filming. She told me that a few weeks after we left, she woke up about three in the morning to an evil presence, that felt female in nature. She began to pray and it started to go away, but then she began to lose her foothold. She thought she was losing the battle. Then, she suddenly saw my face, and I was praying for her. The malevolent entity disappeared. I stopped praying, and she was able to sleep in peace.

Prayer is your most powerful weapon. A simple conversation asking for help works. In this chapter I have included some additional prayers, songs, and psalms that I also use.

Hedge Prayer.[15]

I never do a cleansing without saying a hedge of protection prayer. Its origins lie in the book of Job, where Satan asks the Lord, "Have you not put a hedge around him and his house and all that he has, on every side?" (Job 1:10, ESV). In the Old Testament, a hedge made of thorn bushes was used for keeping livestock contained. It was useful because it could not be breached easily by wild animals. The prayer asks God for a hedge of protection around us to keep us save from evil.

The following is an example of a hedge prayer:

Father,

In the name of Jesus, we lift up _____ to You and pray a hedge of protection around him/her. We thank You, Father, that You are a wall of fire round about _____ and that you set Your angels round about him/her.

---

[15] https://www.living-prayers.com/petitions/
hedge_of_protection_prayer.html#ixzz63O3yDvNG

We thank You, Father, that _____ dwells in the secret place of the Most High and abides under the shadow of the Almighty. We say of You, Lord, You are his/her refuge and fortress, in You will he/she trust. You cover _____ with Your feathers, and under Your wings shall he/she trust. _____ shall not be afraid of the terror by night or the arrow that flies by day. Only with his/her eyes will _____ behold and see the reward of the wicked.

Because _____ has made You, Lord, his/her refuge and fortress, no evil shall befall him/her—no accident will overtake him/her—neither shall any plague or calamity come near him/her. For you give Your angels charge over _____, to keep him/her in all Your ways.

Father, because You have set Your love upon _____, therefore will You deliver him/her. _____ shall call upon You, and You will answer him/her. You will be with him/her in trouble and will satisfy _____ with a long life and show him/her Your salvation. Not a hair of his/her head shall perish.

Amen.

Pre-cleanse Hedge Prayer and Visualization Exercise.[16]

Father,

I nestle into your presence, your love is like a huge wing of protection, encircling my vulnerabilities, gathering up my tired my mind beneath the warmth of your hold and the gentleness of your embrace. Here I remain, hidden in the holy sanctuary of your kingdom, finding a home where I can be real and a harbor from the storms.

You will never reject me, never turn me away, never let me go. I have found my dwelling place, bathed in the light of your grace, drifting with the ebb and flow of your mercy.

I let my fears trickle away, my anxious thoughts cease, my struggles melt away. I am safe in your eternal arms. I trust in the heartbeat of Heaven and know that you will send angels to protect me. I am yours, known and precious, no matter how the world treats me or values me. I know my worth because you paid such a high price for me.

Thank you. Amen.

---

[16] https://www.living-prayers.com/petitions/hedge_of_protection_prayer.html

Prayer to St. Michael
St. Michael the Archangel, defend us in battle;
be our defense against the wickedness and
snares of the devil.
May God rebuke him, we humbly pray;
and do you, O prince of the Heavenly host,
by the power of God,
thrust into Hell, Satan and the other evil spirits
who prowl about the world for the ruin of
souls.
Amen.

The Lord's Prayer.
(From Luke 11: 2-4):
Our Father, who art in heaven,
hallowed be thy name;
thy kingdom come;
thy will be done;
on earth as it is in Heaven.
Give us this day our daily bread.
And forgive us our trespasses,
as we forgive those who trespass against us.
And lead us not into temptation;
but deliver us from evil.
For thine is the kingdom,
the power and the glory,
for ever and ever.

Amen.

Prayer to Saint Benedict for Protection[17]

Saint Benedict (547 A.D.) is the patron saint of those dealing with the occult.

Oh, glorious Saint Benedict, sublime model of all virtues, pure deposit of the grace of God! Here I am, humbly prostrate before you. I implore your heart full of love, that you may intercede for me before the throne of God.

I turn to you in all the dangers that surround me. Protect me from my enemies, from evil enemy in all its forms, and inspire me to imitate you in all things.

May your blessing be with me always, so that I may escape everything that is not pleasing to God and thus avoid the opportunities of sin.

I beseech you tenderly to obtain from God the favors and graces that I so much need in the trials, miseries and afflictions of life.

---

[17] https://www.catholicletters.com/prayer-to-saint-benedict-to-ward-off-evil-and-seek-protection-from-danger/

Your heart has always been so full of love, compassion and mercy to the afflicted or to those with problems of any kind.

You have never dismissed yourself without consolation or help to anyone who has come to you. Therefore, I invoke your powerful intercession, in the hope that you will hear my prayers and grant me special grace in favor of what I so earnestly ask you to do, if it is for the glory of God and for the good of my soul.

Help me, O great Saint Benedict, to live and die as a faithful son of God. May I always be submissive to His holy will in order to attain the eternal happiness of Heaven. Amen.

Scripture Against Evil

Psalm 91 (King James Version)

1 He that dwelleth in the secret place of the most High shall abide under the shadow of the Almighty. 2 I will say of the Lord, He is my refuge and my fortress: my God; in Him will I trust. 3 Surely He shall deliver thee from the snare of the fowler, and from the noisome pestilence. 4 He shall cover thee with His feathers, and under His wings shalt thou trust: His truth shall be

thy shield and buckler. 5 Thou shalt not be afraid for the terror by night; nor for the arrow that flieth by day; 6 Nor for the pestilence that walketh in darkness; nor for the destruction that wasteth at noonday. 7 A thousand shall fall at thy side, and ten thousand at thy right hand; but it shall not come nigh thee. 8 Only with thine eyes shalt thou behold and see the reward of the wicked. 9 Because thou hast made the Lord, which is my refuge, even the most High, thy habitation; 10 There shall no evil befall thee, neither shall any plague come nigh thy dwelling. 11 For He shall give His angels charge over thee, to keep thee in all thy ways. 12 They shall bear thee up in their hands, lest thou dash thy foot against a stone. 13 Thou shalt tread upon the lion and adder: the young lion and the dragon shalt thou trample under feet. 14 Because He hath set His love upon me, therefore will I deliver him: I will set Him on high, because He hath known my name. 15He shall call upon me, and I will answer him: I will be with Him in trouble; I will deliver Him, and honor Him. 16 With long life will I satisfy Him, and shew Him my salvation.

Ephesians 6:12-14, 24 (King James Version)

12 For we wrestle not against flesh and blood, but against principalities, against powers,

against the rulers of the darkness of the world against spiritual wickedness in high places. 13 Wherefore take unto you the whole armour of God, that ye may be able to withstand in the evil day, and having done all, to stand. 24 Grace be with all them that love our Lord Jesus Christ in sincerity.

Amen.

Psalm 27 :1-2, 12 (King James Version)

1 The Lord is my light and my salvation; whom shall I fear? The Lord is the strength of my life; of whom shall I be afraid? 2 When the wicked, even mine enemies and my foes, came upon me to eat up my flesh, they stumbled and fell. 3 Deliver me not over unto the will of mine enemies: for false witnesses are risen up against me, and such as breathe out cruelty.

Nahum 1:7 (King James Version)

The Lord is good, a strong hold in the day of trouble; and He knoweth them that trust in Him. The Lord is good, a strong hold in the day of trouble; and He knoweth them that trust in Him.

Psalm 34 (King James Version)

1 I will bless the Lord at all times: His praise shall continually be in my mouth. 2 My

soul shall make her boast in the   Lord: the humble shall hear thereof, and be glad. 3 O magnify the   Lord with me, and let us exalt His name together. 4I sought the Lord, and He heard me, and delivered me from all my fears. 5 They looked unto Him, and were lightened: and their faces were not ashamed. 6 This poor man cried, and the Lord heard him, and saved him out of all his troubles. 7 The angel of the Lord encampeth round about them that fear him, and delivereth them. 8O taste and see that the Lord is good: blessed is the man that trusteth in Him. 9 O fear the Lord, ye his saints: for there is no want to them that fear Him. 10 The young lions do lack, and suffer hunger: but they that seek the Lord shall not want any good thing.11 Come, ye children, hearken unto me: I will teach you the fear of the Lord. 12 What man is he that desireth life, and loveth many days, that he may see good? 13 Keep thy tongue from evil, and thy lips from speaking guile.14 Depart from evil, and do good; seek peace, and pursue it. 15The eyes of the Lord are upon the righteous, and His ears are open unto their cry. 16 The face of the Lord is against them that do evil, to cut off the remembrance of them from the earth. [17] The righteous cry, and the Lord heareth, and delivereth them out of all their troubles. [18] The Lord is nigh unto them that are of a broken heart; and saveth such as be of a contrite spirit. [19] Many are the afflictions of the righteous: but the Lord delivereth him out of them all. [20] He keepeth all his bones: not one of them is broken. [21] Evil shall slay the wicked: and they that hate the righteous shall be desolate. [22] The Lord redeemeth the soul of His servants: and none of them that trust in Him shall be desolate.

Psalm 23 (King James Version)

[1] The Lord is my shepherd; I shall not want. [2] He maketh me to lie down in green pastures: He leadeth me beside the still waters. [3] He restoreth my soul: He leadeth me in the paths of righteousness for His name's sake. [4] Yea, though I walk through the valley of the shadow of death, I will fear no evil: for thou art with me; thy rod and thy staff they comfort me. [5] Thou preparest a table before me in the presence of mine enemies: thou anointest my head with oil; my cup runneth over. [6] Surely goodness and mercy shall follow me all the days of my life: and I will dwell in the house of the Lord for ever.

Scripture of Praise

I have found that negative entities do not like anything I say which praises God. After I say hedge prayers, I loudly praise the Lord and call on angels. Over and over I praise God and say the Lord's prayer. You may feel a battle ensue, but do not stop. Sometimes I have seen angels carry off gnarled creatures, and other times they flee on their own. I have never doubted, and it has always worked.

Psalm 100 (King James Version)
[1] Make a joyful noise unto the Lord, all ye lands. [2] Serve the Lord with gladness: come before his presence with singing. [3] Know ye that the Lord He is God: it is He that hath made us, and not we ourselves; we are His people, and the sheep of His pasture. [4] Enter into His gates with thanksgiving, and into His courts with praise: be thankful unto Him, and bless his name. [5] For the Lord is good; His mercy is everlasting; and His truth endureth to all generations.

Psalm 150 (King James Version)
[1] Praise ye the Lord. Praise God in His sanctuary; praise Him in the firmament of His power. [2] Praise Him for his mighty acts: praise Him

according to his excellent greatness. 3 Praise Him with the sound of the trumpet: praise Him with the psaltery and harp. 4 Praise Him with the timbrel and dance: praise Him with stringed instruments and organs.5Praise Him upon the high-sounding cymbals. 6Let every thing that hath breath praise the Lord. Praise ye the Lord.

Psalm 33: 1-10, 18-22 (King James Version)

1 Rejoice in the Lord, O ye righteous: for praise is comely for the upright. 2 Praise the Lord with harp: sing unto Him with the psaltery and an instrument of ten strings. 3 Sing unto Him a new song; play skillfully with a loud noise. 4 For the word of the Lord is right; and all His works are done in truth. 5 He loveth righteousness and judgment: the earth is full of the goodness of the Lord. 6 By the word of the Lord were the heavens made; and all the host of them by the breath of His mouth. 7 He gathereth the waters of the sea together as an heap: He layeth up the depth in storehouses. 8 Let all the earth fear the Lord: let all the inhabitants of the world stand in awe of Him. 9 For he spake, and it was done; He commanded, and it stood fast. 10 The Lord bringeth the counsel of the heathen to nought: He maketh the devices of the people of none effect.

¹⁸ Behold, the eye of the Lord is upon them that fear Him, upon them that hope in His mercy; ¹⁹ To deliver their soul from death, and to keep them alive in famine. ²⁰ Our soul waiteth for the Lord: He is our help and our shield. ²¹ For our heart shall rejoice in Him, because we have trusted in His holy name. ²² Let thy mercy, O Lord, be upon us, according as we hope in thee.

Pagan Prayer

Prayer to Goddess[18]

O' Gracious Goddess of love and light
Protect me now with all thy might.
Watch over me and mine with care,
So that we may avoid dangerous snares.

Hail Fair Goddess,
Protector of the night.
Banish all evil from my sight.
Send it far and away from me.
So it is and so mote it be.

---

[18] https://www.moonlightmessages.com/magick-and-spells/prayers-and-chants

10.

RESOURCES

The Investigative Medium Series by Laine Crosby.

Book 1: *Investigative Medium—the Awakening*
Book 2: *The Adventures of a Free-Range Psychic Medium* (Expected 2020)

Prayers.

Armor of God: Prayers for Protection and Deliverance by Dave Juliano

Demons.

The Encyclopedia of Demons and Demonology by Rosemary Ellen Guiley and John Zaffis

Demon Haunted: True Stories from the John Zaffis Vault Kindle Edition by John Zaffis and Rosemary Ellen Guiley

The Vengeful Djinn: Unveiling the Hidden Agenda of Genies by Rosemary Ellen Guiley and Philip J. Imbrogno

Personal Protection from occultism and folk magic.

Guide to Psychic Protection by Rosemary Ellen Guiley

Spells8.com/protection-spells-recipes/

Angels.

The Encyclopedia of Angels
by Rosemary Guiley and Lisa Schwebel

Angels by Billy Graham

What happens when we die?
Beginning in1912, journalist Elsa Barker channeled
a man she had once met, named Judge Hatch. She
began doing automatic writing, and eventually he
dictated the following trilogy about the afterlife.

Letters from a Living Dead Man
(Also called *Letters from the Afterlife: A Guide to
the Other Side*)
War Letters From a Living Dead Man
Last Letters From The Living Dead Man

Excerpt from
Investigative Medium–the
Awakening

It was the morning of September 21, 2004, and I sat on my deck overlooking the lake and rolling hills of Rock Creek Park, thinking of the plantation that once was. I could see several dark skinned men in the field with straw hats, white shirts, and suspenders. After another sip of tea, they were gone.

It was quiet. In Atlanta, I could always hear the sound of I-75, and the noise of the city, but I had never heard the flawless sound of silence as I do here. I remembered my excitement to spend our first night in our new home, until I realized it was too noiseless to sleep, and my first stop the next day had been the Home Depot for a white noise machine.

I have wasted enough time this morning dreaming about what once was. I only had one more box to unpack and my domestic duties would be history too. By now, it was almost lunchtime and Chris would come through the door for his peanut butter and jelly sandwich with potato chips separating the layers for added crunch.

As I leaned over to pull the crock pot out of the last box, the only thing I pulled out was my back. At first it was only a noise, then I tried to move. Chris soon found me on the floor, as well as the humor in the situation. I had moved dressers and sofas, and lugged the twins on either hip, but a crock pot had gotten the best of me. He helped me into bed, kissed me on the forehead, made his PB&J, and left for work.

My best friend in nearby Alexandria, Virginia, had already moved with her husband to another Air Force base, and I calculated my nearest friend was six hundred and twenty-four miles away. But somehow, I didn't feel lonely. Or rather, I didn't feel alone.

I drifted off to sleep for minutes, or hours maybe, until I heard the sweet, soft voice of a woman. Her voice was louder than the other voices in my dream, and I started to become restless from the sound.

"I had a son the same age as yours," I heard clearly.

In my delirious state of mind, it seemed natural to chat with this woman, but as I started to awaken, reality began to manifest, and I was confused. Does she think my son is hers? Is she confused? Or am I confused? Who am I talking to?

"He is my son and not yours," I said, and as quickly as those words addressed her in my mind, I realized I sounded a bit unbalanced.

After a pause, I heard a compassionate voice say, "I know he is your son."

I am waking up much more quickly now, and I perceive a presence beside my head. I see the image of a beautiful woman with dark skin and an almond shaped face. She is simple and soulful and composed. She defined beauty.

"What is your name?" I inquire.

"Janette."

I am wide awake now and I see her smile at me, then her voice and mirage fade away into nothingness. Whoa. I just made contact.

Long after the twins had returned from school and had gone to bed, I asked Chris to blank his mind for a moment and meditate to see if he heard anything. I could feel his agitation growing. Although he knew I wasn't crazy, he was becoming too upset to humor me for long, but kindly, he remained quiet and closed his eyes.

I felt the same presence, the same energy or "feeling" as when the woman had visited me earlier, and I concentrated hard to see if I could hear anything.

"I pat his hair at night. He reminds me of the man I once loved."

I gasped! At once I knew it was Janette. "Did you hear anything, Chris?", I asked.

"Nothing."

"It was the woman again. You have an admirer! I knew it was Janette. She said she touches your hair at night because she was in love with a man who looked just like you."

The next morning, I surfed the Internet for local history. I found a historical society, but it seemed to be a long shot. I sank into the sofa, hopeless, but I knew better than to give up. My father and I had climbed mountains and hiked through snakes, fox holes and chiggers to do our genealogical research, and nothing could be as hard as spending my childhood summers scrubbing tombstones in the heat of the South.

I suddenly see a picture in my head of rows of slave cabins, and a mansion, or what folks here call a "manor home." I felt the same presence again and knew I was being led somewhere and an explanation was forthcoming. The urge to leave my house grew stronger, as if I were late to an important event. Since I had no plans, I knew the feeling was imposed on me, and I was absorbing it.

Precisely at the moment I had planned to leave, Chris arrives for his PB&J. Another delay, and the feeling was growing more pronounced. The moment he left, I sprung to my Chevy Blazer and drove to the end of our driveway. I assumed I would be told where to go, and I was strangely excited to feel the compulsion to turn right. Somehow, I was beginning to understand that which was outside my comprehension.

I drove slowly for half a mile, awaiting the inevitable feeling of my next move. On the left I saw subdivisions of recently built homes, and on the right was still Rock Creek Park. A long drive came into view, confined by a row of majestic loblolly pines on each side, which even in this century, seem to oblige a manor home. I turned down the drive, a little nervous about trespassing, and wondered what I would say if confronted. The house was the same as it had been in my vision, although I did not remember driving in this direction previously. There were no stores, restaurants or schools, just rolling hills, lakes, and the mammoth Rock Creek Park which extends from the district all the way through Maryland toward Pennsylvania.

The drive turned to the left just in front of the home, and into a small parking lot on the side. I felt more comfortable knowing that the mansion housed a business, and I might be able to find some answers.

I hurriedly parked and turned to walk to the front door, when in my peripheral vision, I caught a sight that rendered me speechless. I turned to see what looked like slave cabins directly behind the house, the very same cabins I had been shown in my vision. I grew cold and could feel every hair, electrified. I carefully walked behind the house, and I could see flat grassland next to these cabins, as if there had once been many more.

My left side became hot and I knew I was not alone. In my head I said, "I know you are here. Is this where you lived?" I heard simply, "yes".

I may have run to the front of the house. Perhaps I rang the bell and knocked so loudly that everyone in the house knew I had arrived; I hardly recall. A handsome middle-aged man opened the door and said, "Yes?"

I have never talked faster than when I blurted, "Hi! My name is Laine Crosby, and I just moved into the yellow house..." and I flung my arm to point west and continued, "and I want to know..." and I paused as I looked around the door for a sign and said, "What is this place anyway?"

The man responded, "These are the offices for the county department of parks and recreation, and I'm Mike, the historian".

"Wonderful!" I gushed. "...then I need your help. Can you tell me what happened here on this property? I mean, a long time ago, what went on here and where I live?" The man began, "Well," and I interrupted, "You see, I have ghosts. There are people in my house, and I know this sounds crazy, but I promise I'm not. I want to know what happened because there are voices talking to me of people I can't see."

Mike looked at me incredulously. I couldn't tell whether he thought I would be a danger if he opened the door, or if he were concerned for me.

Mike asked, "How long have you been here?"

"Only a minute or two," I replied

He pointed down the driveway to a local news affiliate van and said, "Were you here when that woman was here?"

"No, I just came."

"Well, she was filming a story for Halloween about our ghosts here. Lots of people around here see them. Come on in and wait here, I want you to talk to someone."

Mike disappeared up the stairs of this stately edifice, and I entered the grand foyer. I imagined children running and giggling, and a piano playing. I was brought back into the moment when the old grandfather clock struck 1:00 p.m.

As I turned to admire its design, I caught a glimpse of an old picture from the mid-1800s, hanging on the wall. I leaned forward and squinted for a closer look, and cold chills ran up my spine.

My husband's face was staring back at me.

Investigative Medium–the Awakening is available in paperback on Amazon, and as an ebook at online retailers.[19] To learn more about Laine and her books, visit LaineCrosby.com.

---

[19] https://www.amazon.com/Laine-Crosby/e/B00DUJ07KQ?
ref=sr_ntt_srch_lnk_1&qid=1572914894&sr=8-1

ABOUT THE AUTHOR

LAINE CROSBY

LAINE CROSBY is an investigative medium and author of several books including the *New York Times* Bestseller and #1 Amazon Bestseller, I*nvestigative Medium–the Awakening*, about her own true story. Laine moved to a Maryland plantation and awakened suddenly psychic, talking to the spirit of a slave buried in her yard.

As the daughter of Atlanta Civil War Author/Historian, C.P. Crosby, Laine developed a love of history and writing early in life and has worked with law enforcement, forensic scientists, detectives, missing persons networks, historians, and archaeologists to find out what history has not revealed.

Currently, Laine can be seen on the Travel Channel's *Ghost Brothers: Haunted Houseguests* and has appeared on other shows on the Travel Channel, Biography Channel, and FYI networks. She has been featured in *The Washington Post*, *San Francisco Chronicle*, and numerous other local and national papers, radio shows, news and local television segments. Her work has also been featured in dozens of books, including those by Historians Dennis Hocker and Mark Nesbitt, a true-crime anthology by Detective Lee Loftlan, and other works by Forensic Psychologist, Dr. Katherine Ramsland.

Laine also consults with production companies developing paranormal shows for national cable television networks.

Laine holds a B.A. in Economics from Agnes Scott College, and an M.B.A. from Georgia State University, among other graduate certificates and professional certifications. Laine is a member of the Daughters of the American Revolution, and Americans of Royal Descent. She is a journalist and award-winning editor of a national magazine that serves the banking industry.

Laine is a native of Atlanta, Georgia and currently lives in Derwood, Maryland with her husband Chris, twins Annie and Caleb, and Jack Russell terrier Pete. She loves reading, writing, Georgia Tech football, and exploring historic sites.

Visit LaineCrosby.com for more books, tv shows, and appearances.